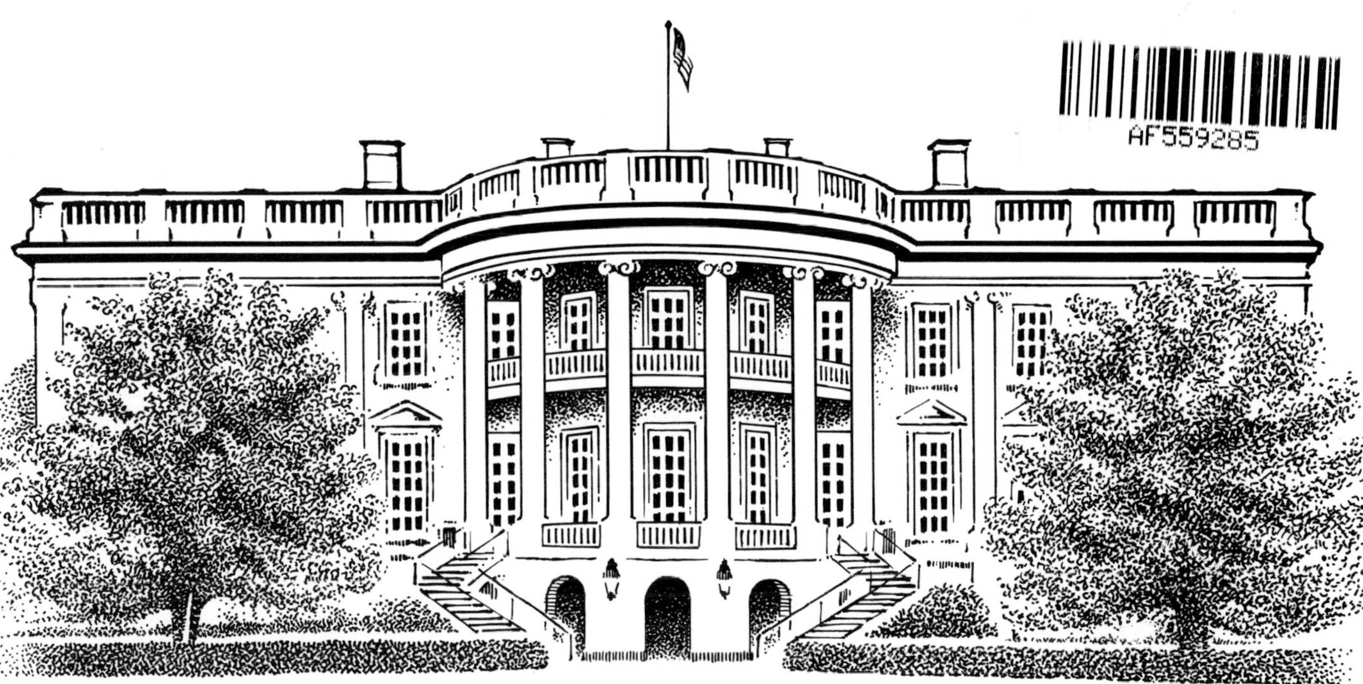

The White House, Washington, D.C.

Monticello, Virginia

Mount Vernon, Virginia

San Francisco

The Statue of Liberty, New York City

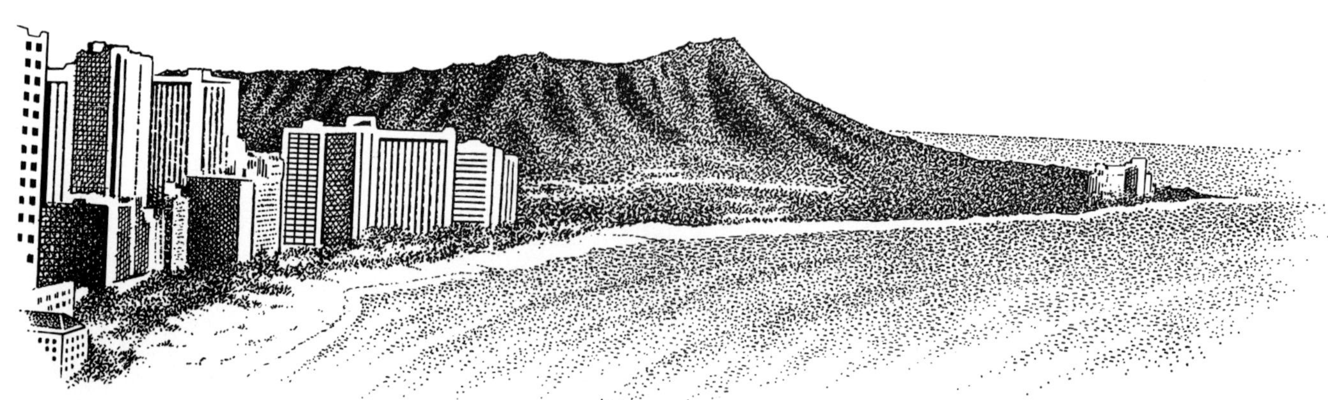

Diamond Head, Hawaii

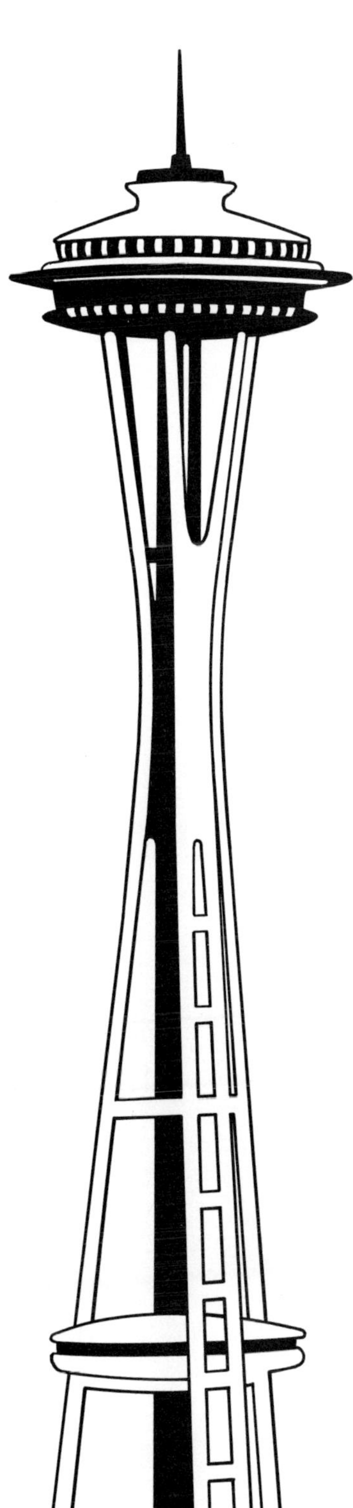

Space Needle, Seattle

Faneuil Hall, Boston

Vieux Carré, New Orleans

Old State House, Boston

Bethesda Fountain, New York City

Mount Rushmore National Memorial, South Dakota

Brooklyn Bridge, New York City

State House, Boston

Empire State Building, New York City

The Capitol, Washington, D.C.

Riverboat, Mississippi River

Louisburg Square, Boston

Jefferson Memorial, Washington, D.C.

World Trade Center and Battery Park City, New York City

Lincoln Memorial, Washington, D.C.

Grand Canyon, Arizona

Chicago

Hollywood sign, Los Angeles

Gateway Arch, St. Louis

Niagara Falls, New York/Canada

Old Faithful, Yellowstone National Park, Wyoming

Redwood trees, California

New York Public Library

Washington Monument, Washington, D.C.

Jackson Square, New Orleans

The Alamo, San Antonio

Trinity Church, Boston

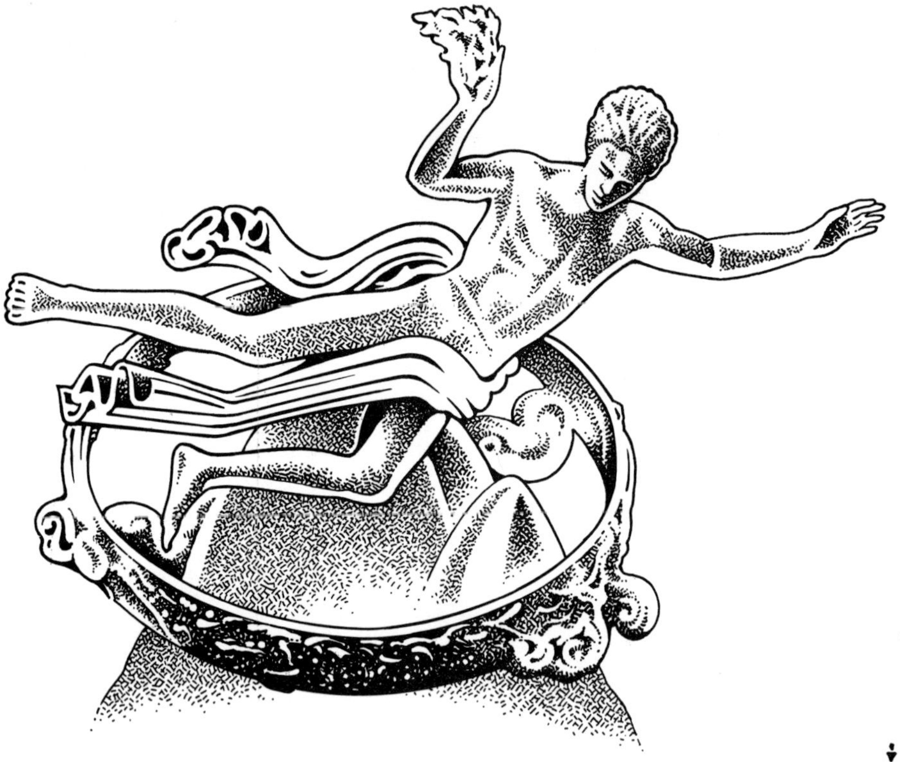

Prometheus, Rockefeller Center, New York City

Independence Hall, Philadelphia

Public Garden, Boston

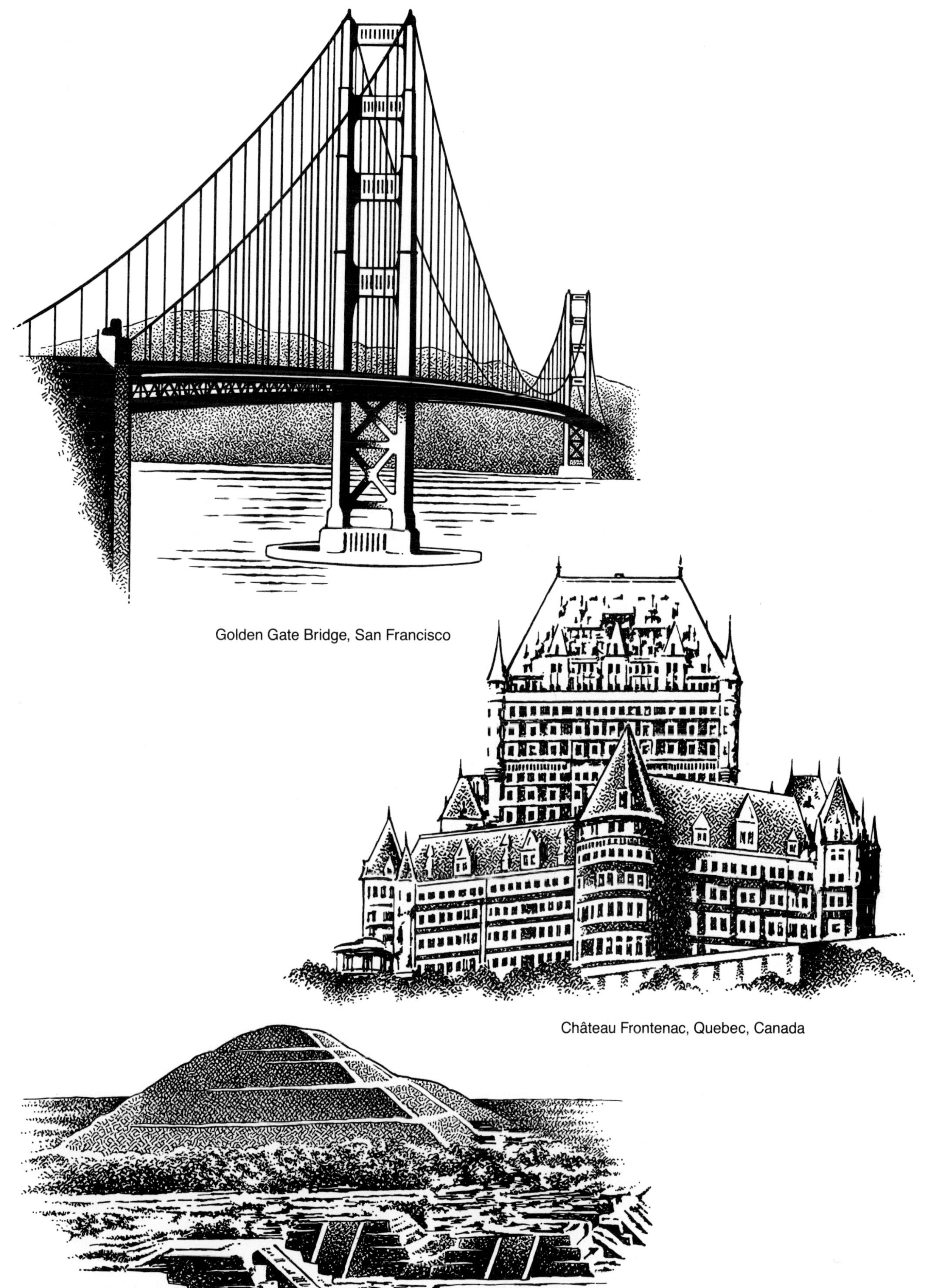

Golden Gate Bridge, San Francisco

Château Frontenac, Quebec, Canada

Pyramid of the Sun, Teotihuacán, Mexico

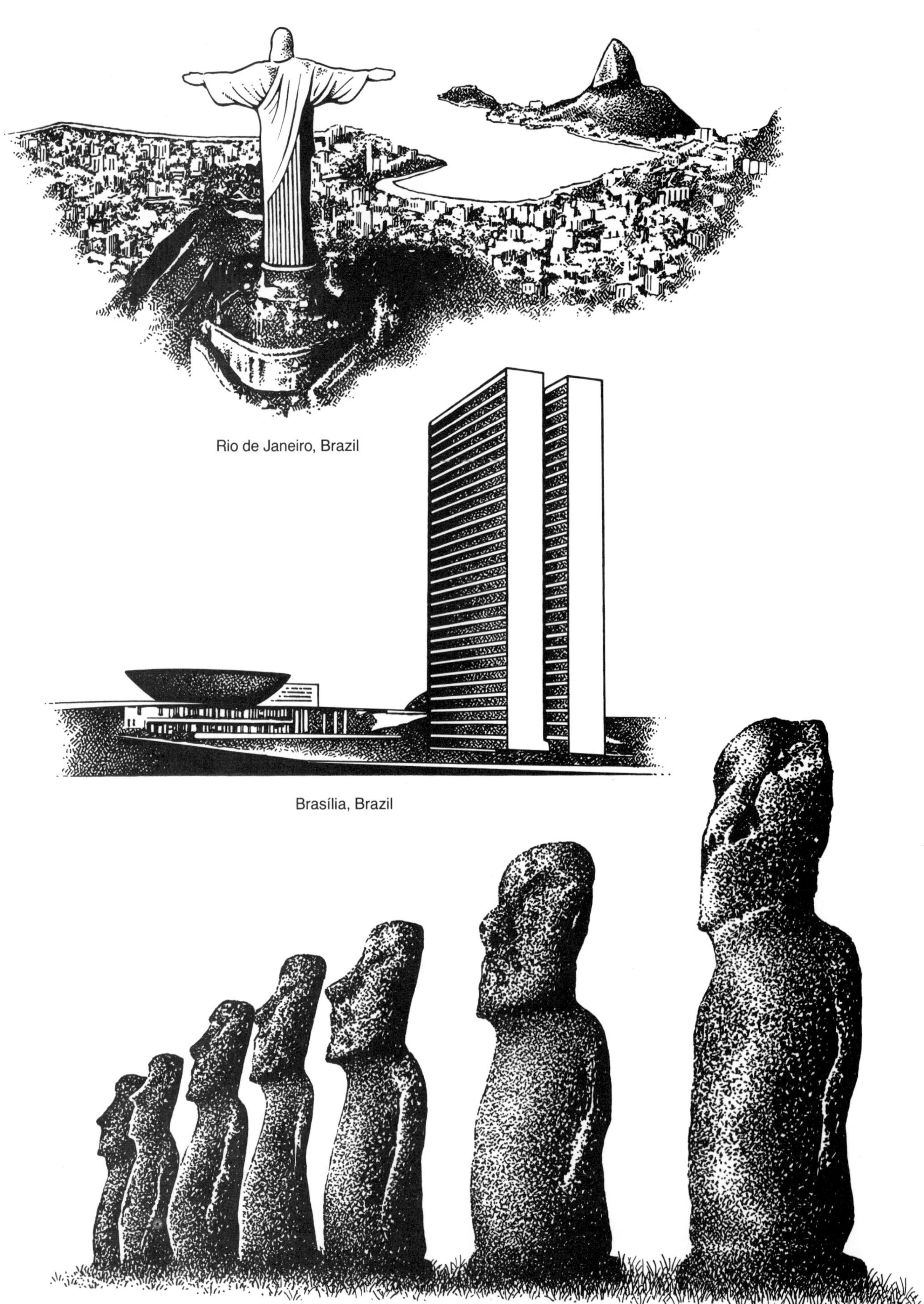

Rio de Janeiro, Brazil

Brasília, Brazil

Easter Island statues, Chile

Stonehenge, England

St. Paul's Cathedral, London

Westminster Abbey, London

Tower of London

Trafalgar Square, London

Houses of Parliament, London

Piccadilly Circus, London

Edinburgh Castle, Scotland

Blarney Castle, Ireland

Arc de Triomphe, Paris

Opéra (Palais Garnier), Paris

Versailles, France

Sacré-Cœur, Paris

Chartres Cathedral, France

Notre-Dame Cathedral, Paris

Eiffel Tower, Paris

Amsterdam, The Netherlands

Little Mermaid statue, Copenhagen, Denmark

Fjord, Norway

Old Town, Stockholm, Sweden

Innsbruck, Austria

St. Stephen's Cathedral, Vienna

Karlskirche, Vienna

Staatsoper, Vienna

Neuschwanstein Castle, Germany

Brandenburg Gate, Berlin

Matterhorn, Switzerland

Ponte Vecchio, Florence

Bay of Naples/Mount Vesuvius

The Duomo, Milan

Leaning Tower of Pisa

Trevi Fountain, Rome

Piazza San Marco, Venice

Colosseum, Rome

St. Peter's, Rome

Palazzo Vecchio, Florence

Rialto Bridge, Venice

The Forum, Rome

Castel Sant'Angelo, Rome

Spanish Steps, Rome

Bridge of Sighs, Venice

Alcázar, Segovia, Spain

Alhambra Palace, Granada, Spain

Tower of Belém, Lisbon, Portugal

Hagia Sophia, Istanbul, Turkey

The Parthenon, Athens

Delphi, Greece

St. Sophia Cathedral, Novgorod, Russia

St. Basil's Cathedral, Moscow

Winter Palace, St. Petersburg, Russia

The Kremlin, Moscow

Wailing Wall, Jerusalem

Temple Mount, Jerusalem

Abu Simbel, Egypt

Great Sphinx/Pyramids, Egypt

Temple of Karnak, Egypt

Mount Kilimanjaro, Kenya

Taj Mahal, India

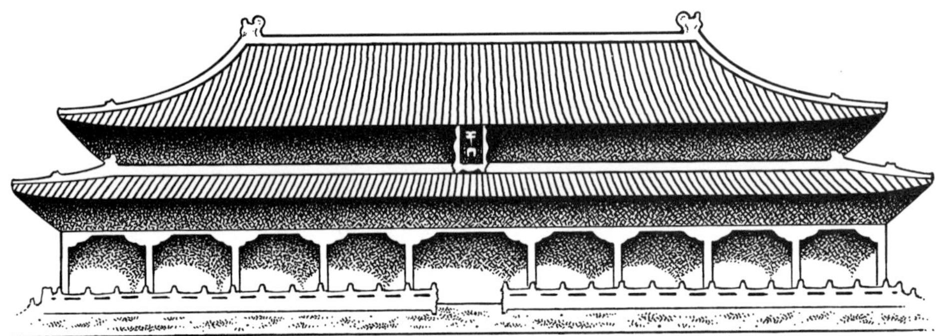

Forbidden City, Beijing, China

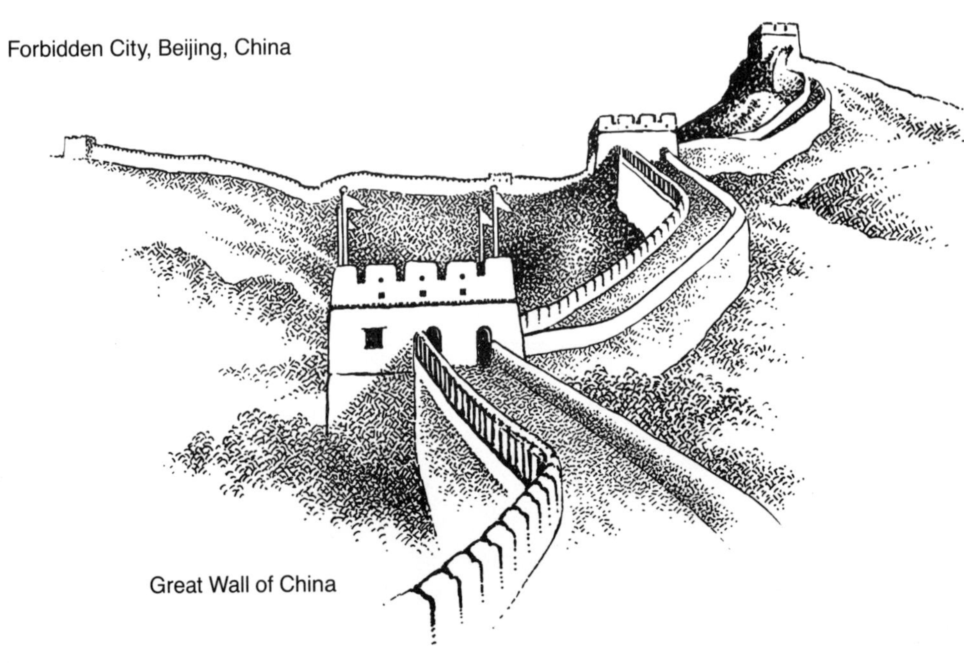

Great Wall of China

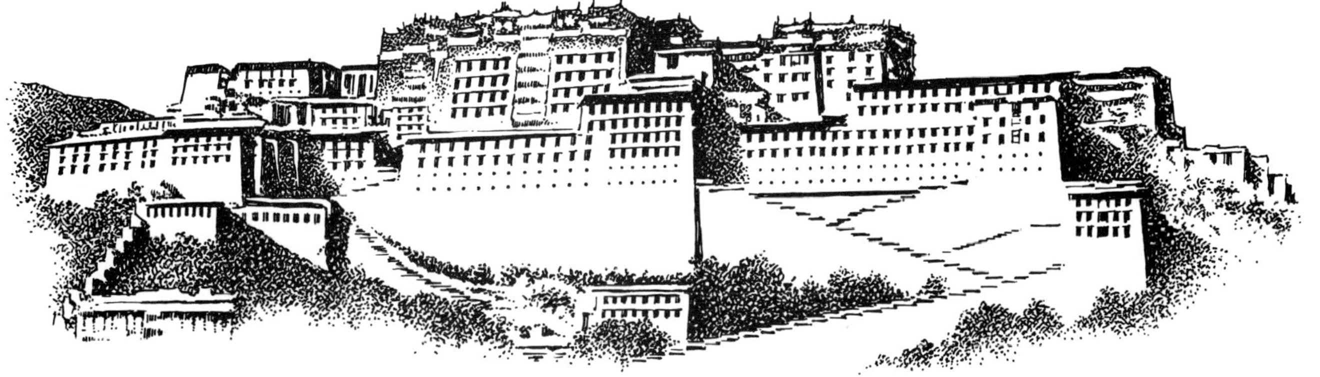

Potala Palace, Lhasa, Tibet

Angkor Wat, Cambodia

Sydney Opera House, Australia

Golden Pavilion, Kyoto, Japan

Buddha statue (Daibutsu), Kamakura, Japan

Mount Fuji, Japan

Osaka Castle, Japan